A CIP catalogue record for this book is available from the British Library.

Many thanks to Gary, Clair, Alan and the Trustees for their much-appreciates support for the Storytelling Group at Shenehom.

And thanks to all friends of Shenehom.

THE SHENEHOM COLLECTION

Drama and poetry from the residents of Shenehom Care-home in West London.

The Shenehom Storytelling Group is a generic creative endeavour guided by the artistic instincts of the residents of Shenehom Care-home in Barnes. To begin with the group was centred ideas to interactive groups based on the creative spontaneity of Gestalt and used cartoons and illustrations to frame and celebrate aspects of residents' lives. The format was very much about being in the moment and celebrating the moment. Humour, solidarity and trust were the founding precepts of the group.

As we went on we began to look at the possibility of a dramatic rendition of content we liked. Then we agreed we would do some kind of creative

performance. But what kind of creative performance? Firstly we looked at classic texts and discussed whether it'd be a good idea to abridge a classic text and then read it in the group. We looked at a few texts and then we'd an idea to write our own scripts and make them relevant to life at Shenehom. This we did.

Closing Time was performed at the Old Sorting Office Theatre in West London in September 2021.

Staff joined in and acted in the production alongside residents.

The theme of the play was to do with the implications of closing institutions and replacing hospital care with the controversial policy of care in the community.

CLOSING TIME

BY THE SHENEHOM STORYTELLING GROUP

BENNY – THOMAS

BESSIE – MARGARITA

BIBI - DENISE

BERYL -JUDY

NURSE PAYNE – Alan

DOCTOR PROCTOR – Clair

THE SURVEYOR: Gary

SCENE ONE: A hospital day-room.

BENNY IS PACING TO AND FRO, PAUSING AT
TIMES AS IF DEEP IN THOUGHT. BESSIE AND
BIBI ARE SITTING DOING A JIGSAW PUZZLE.

BESSIE: Raise the sails against the North wind!

BIBI: I would if I had a boat.

BESSIE: Porcelain ginger jar, porcelain ginger
jar.

BIBI: How long have we been doing this jigsaw
puzzle?

BESSIE: We started before Christmas.

BIBI: Almost a year then.

BESSIE: Christmas 2007.

BIBI: Really. Years and years ago.

BESSIE: Yes, years and years ago. But you'll have to admit it's a hard jigsaw puzzle.

BIBI: We've been doing this for too long. We should move onto something new.

BESSIE: Something new? Is that wise?

BIBI: Benny, do you think we should move onto something new?

BENNY PAUSE FROM HIS CONTANT PACING TO CONSIDER BIBI'S QUESTION.

BENNY: Well ... I would say it'll probably get worse before it gets better.

BIBI: I thought you'd say that.

BENNY CONTINUES PACING, BIBI AND BESSIE
CONTINUE LOOKING AT THE JIGSAW PIECES
IN FRONT OF THEM.

BERYL ENTERS

BESSIE: Hi Beryl.

BERYL: Hi Bessie.

BIBI: Hi Beryl.

BERYL: Hi Bibi. Hi Benny.

BENNY PAUSES, LOOKS TOWARDS BERYL AS
IF PUZZLED BY HER ENTRY. NODS.
CONTINUES PACING.

BESSIE: Beryl, do you think Bibi and I have
been doing this jigsaw for too long?

BERYL: How many years is it now?

BESSIE: We've lost count.

BIBI: We were thinking about moving onto something new.

BESSIE: I don't think we should rush into it.

BERYL: Maybe you should rush into it. I've got a letter from my social worker. I can read it to you.

BESSIE: Do you have to?

BERYL: Benny could you please stop pacing up and down. This is of interest to you too.

BENNY: Yes that's what I was saying earlier. It'll probably get worse before it gets better.

BERYL: The letter reads. Dear Beryl, as you're probably aware Chase Hospital is closing soon and patients will be moving into the community where possible. As your care-co-ordinator I'm confident of placing you either at the Menzies cluster or at Canbury Street where I will continue to support you and where you'll have an off-site warden to respond to emergencies if required. I know you're ready to return to the community and I know the community is ready for you. Take heart, it's all for the good I'm sure. I know you've spent a long time at Chase and you've made so many friends there. But it is a hospital and we don't really wish to live in a hospital for very long do we? I'll be visiting soon so we can talk it all through in more detail.

All the very best. Brandi Rockets.

Gosh. It looks like we'll all be out on the road soon.

BENNY: Yes, I thought as much. It'll definitely get worse before it gets better.

ENTER DOCTOR PROCTOR AND NURSE PAYNE

DOCTOR PROCTOR: Hi. How's everyone?

BERYL: Hi Doctor Proctor. Have you heard? We'll all be out on the road very soon.

DOCTOR PROCTOR: Don't think it's that bad, is it?

NURSE PAYNE: How are you today Benny?

BENNY: I'm okay Nurse Payne.

NURSE PAYNE: Has it got worse yet, before it's got better?

BENNY: Not that I've noticed. But give it time.

BERYL: My social worker Brandi Rockets said we'll all be out on the road soon.

DOCTOR PROCTOR: Hardly Beryl, hardly.

NURSE PAYNE: So ladies, still working on the old jigsaw puzzle?

BESSIE: Nurse Payne, do you think we've been working on this jigsaw for too long?

NURSE PAYNE: No. There's another few years left in it yet.

DOCTOR PROCTOR: By the way Nurse Payne, did you manage to get those appraisals done?

NURSE PAYNE: Actually, no.

DOCTOR PROCTOR: You haven't?

NURSE PAYNE: So much to do doctor. An entire hospital closing down.

DOCTOR PROCTOR: I had expected them last week.

NURSE PAYNE: Really?

DOCTOR PROCTOR: They've been pending.

NURSE PAYNE: Really?

DOCTOR PROCTOR: They've been pending for so long.

NURSE PAYNE: Yes indeed, pending bending.

DOCTOR PROCTOR: What do you mean pending bending?

NURSE PAYNE: Just a little levity doctor, just a little levity. I promise you I'll have them all done before Bessie and Bibi finish their jigsaw.

DOCTOR PROCTOR: I think we need to discuss the appraisals another time, in private.

BERYL: Doctor Proctor, are you sure we're not getting kicked out on the road?

DOCTOR PROCTOR: Yes, I'm sure. Do we come across as the kind of people who'd kick our patients onto the road?

NURSE PAYNE: You don't have to answer that?

BERYL: Well if the worse comes to the worst I have a bag packed. I guess I could live at the main bus-station in the town for a while.

DOCTOR PROCTOR: Beryl, you'll be fine. We're moving you to another living arrangement. Haven't you been told all that?

NURSE PAYNE: Numerous times.

BERYL: Okay, if you say so.

BESSIE: We mustn't forget anxiety. There will surely be anxiety.

DOCTOR PROCTOR: Nurse Payne, could we have a private word?

NURSE PAYNE: Why not?

DOCTOR PROCTOR: Is everything okay?

NURSE PAYNE: Why wouldn't it be?

DOCTOR PROCTOR: It's just that we're meant to be taking resettlement seriously around here.

NURSE PAYNE: Do we take anything seriously around here?

DOCTOR PROCTOR: What's that supposed to mean?

NURSE PAYNE: Well it's not serious is it, closing down a hospital?

DOCTOR PROCTOR: That's right, the hospital is closing and we're preparing the patients for living in the community.

NURSE PAYNE: There is no community.

DOCTOR PROCTOR: Well that's what they call it, whether there is a community or not.

NURSE PAYNE: It's Orwellian.

DOCTOR PROCTOR: It's reality. The hospital is closing and patients will now be living in supported schemes in the community, or if you prefer living somewhere that isn't a hospital. Our job is make all that happen, to ensure everyone is adequately housed and supported. We've been talking about this more or less continuously for the past two years.

NURSE PAYNE: They'll end up alone, without anything to do. All this is the very opposite to care.

DOCTOR PROCTOR: We've been working towards this end for years.

NURSE PAYNE: And I've been saying it's a terrible idea for years.

DOCTOR PROCTOR: Yes, private opinions cannot be discounted. But our job is to get everyone ready for a life lived outside hospitals.

NURSE PAYNE: Count me out.

DOCTOR PROCTOR: Count you out?

NURSE PAYNE: I just don't buy it, think it's all wrong. We're just passing on our responsibilities to people who are not experienced or qualified enough to deal with any of it.

DOCTOR PROCTOR: It's policy. I need those appraisals.

NURSE PAYNE: I came into nursing to nurse, not to chuck patients who need nursing out into some community that in reality doesn't exist.

DOCTOR PROCTOR: It's the model of mental health care we're conforming to, it's the future.

NURSE PAYNE: I don't want any part in it.

DOCTOR PROCTOR: Really? You don't want any part in it?

NURSE PAYNE: It's the opposite of good care and responsible nursing. Why would I want any part of it?

DOCTOR PROCTOR: We'll need to discuss this with hospital management.

NURSE PAYNE: No. Actually you'll need to discuss this with hospital management.

DOCTOR PROCTOR: I think we should end this conversation.

NURSE PAYNE: Care in the community doesn't work. There's very little care and there's no community as such.

DOCTOR PROCTOR: You can continue this conversation with the head of nursing.

NURSE PAYNE: So you haven't heard then?

DOCTOR PROCTOR: What exactly haven't I heard?

NURSE PAYNE: I'm taking early retirement. So it looks like you'll have to close down the hospital without my help and then sort everyone out in the wonderful community we keep hearing about?

DOCTOR PROCTOR: Nobody told me.

NURSE PAYNE: Good luck then. I'm off.

NURSE PAYNE EXITS

Doctor Proctor looks in the direction Nurse Payne has just gone in, shakes her head and then exists in the opposite direction.

THE SURVEYOR ENTERS, CARRYING A CLIPBOARD AND LOOKING CRITICALLY IN A NUMBER OF DIRECTIONS.

THE SURVEYOR: All right, how is everyone? It's all go gogoaround here then.

BESSIE: Who are you?

THE SURVEYOR: I'm the surveyor love, from Alcock and Upstead.

BESSIE: Cock up and what?

THE SURVEYOR: I said Alcock and Upstead. That's the company I work for. Known all over all London and the Southeast, for all the right reasons of course. I'm here to do a proper survey, to see if there's any part of this old building worth saving. Have a good old gander at the gaff. And straight up without even having to take a closer look I can see there's asbestos up there. That'll have to come down for a start. In fact, most of this old ruin can be pulled down.

BERYL: It's hardly an old ruin. It's a hospital.

BESSIE: It'sourhome.

BIBI: We've lived here for years.

THE SURVEYOR: I'd say it was built sometime around the 1860s. If we didn't bother knocking it down it'd probably fall down all by itself.

BERYL: You're not very sensitive are you? How would you feel if I went to your home and said it looks like it's about to fall down?

THE SURVEYOR: Well firstly love, I can't see any reason why you'd be asked to come to my gaff. And secondly I live in a very large and very expensive house in the Surrey countryside, the kind of house that's hardly about to fall down any day soon.

BESSIE: You're right Beryl, he is insensitive.

BIBI: Very.

THE SURVEYOR: Let's hope English Heritage doesn't stick a preservation order on this old dump. Ideally, we'd like to flatten it to the ground. By the way when are you lot clearing out of here? Pretty soon I hope.

BESSIE: Are you going to knock down the hospital when we're asleep in our beds?

THE SURVEYOR: By the time we get a crane on-site love you'll all be long gone out of here. Having said that, do keep an eye open at night. If you hear the sound of a crane warming up then scarper.

BESSIE: So we can't sleep at night for fear of the building getting knocked down and falling on top of us?

BIBI: That isn't very fair.

BERYL: Maybe you could discuss it with the nurses. We're only patients after all.

THE SURVEYOR: I don't mind talking to a nurse if there's any fit ones about. But there's hardly anyone here. Like rats deserting a ship they are. I'm surprised you lot are still hanging around.

BIBI: You can't knock a hospital down with patients still living in it.

THE SURVEYOR: You never know love, you never know. Strange days we're living in.

BERYL: It's probably best if you went.

THE SURVEYOR: I'll go when I'm good and ready to go.

BESSIE: If there's many people like him in the community I don't want to go there.

THE SURVEYOR: Excuse me mate, do you know where the boiler-room is?

BENNY: I beg your pardon?

THE SURVEYOR: The boiler-room, you know, where they keep the boiler. Do you live here too?

BENNY: Yes I live here, but I don't know where the boiler-room is.

THE SURVEYOR: Just moved in here have you?

BENNY: No, I've been here for years.

THE SURVEYOR: You've been here for years and you don't know where the boiler-room is?

BESSIE: Leave Benny alone. It's not his job to know where the boiler-room is.

THE SURVEYOR: That's all right. I'll find it myself. And by the way, your time here is fast running out. I don't want to see any of you lot here when I return next week. You're getting in the way, slowing things up.

THE SURVEYOR EXITS

BERYL: What an insensitive fellow.

BIBI: A brute.

BESSIE: Is that what people from the community are like.

BERYL: I hope not.

BIBI: If they're all like that I want to stay here.

BESSIE: Too late, they're knocking the hospital down.

BERYL: Oh dear.

BIBI: What are we going to do?

BESSIE: Is it time to panic?

BERYL: Benny, what do you think?

BENNY: Hmmmmmmmm ...

BESSIE: I think we know what Benny's going to say.

BIBI: By the look of things he's probably right.

BIBI/BERYL/BESSIE: It'll definitely get worse before it gets better.

THE END

The Room at the End of the Sea was a ghost story performed at OSO theatre in West London. Margarita V was exceptional in the part of the Ghost and was very well supported by Thomas N as the Villager and Baljit S and Denise R as the Pilgrims.

The Room at the Edge of the Sea

By the Shenehom Storytelling Group

The Villager: Thomas

The Ghost: Margarita

The Guest: Judy

First Pilgrim: Baljit

Second Pilgrim: Denise

SCENE ONE:

The Villager enters, goes to the candle and bell.
Rings the bell. Looks to the right and to the left.

The light should be enough to bring her here.

Waits.

Looks around.

Exits.

SCENE TWO:

First pilgrim enters.

Go to candle and bell.

Throws down money.

Here, I know this is yours. Take it. Give it to someone else.

Exit.

SCENE THREE

Second pilgrim enters.

Rings the bell.

Notices the money. Takes it.

Thank you. Thank you for listening to me.

Exits.

SCENE FOUR

The Guest enters.

Sits.

Picks up a nearby book.

Legend has it that a famous healer haunts this old hotel. People still believe in this old yarn and believe her to be a powerful spirit. They come here to ask favours from her. Can you believe it? How innocent people are.

THE VILLAGER: You surprised me.

THE GUEST: Sorry. Didn't think anyone comes in here. I think I know you.

THE VILLAGER: I'm from this village.

THE GUEST: Yes, I've seen you before.

THE VILLAGER Are you staying here?

THE GUEST: Yes. I stayed here last year as well.

THE VILLAGER: So you like it here?

THE GUEST: Yes, I like it.

THE VILLAGER: Good.

THE GUEST: Do you stay here, at the inn?

THE VILLAGER: No. I clean the gutters. Yesterday I fixed the gate out the back.

THE GUEST: And today?

THE VILLAGER: Today ... I'm in the old guest room.

THE GUEST: This is the old guest-room.

THE VILLAGER: That's right.

THE GUEST: I don't think it's used any longer, at least not for guests.

THE VILLAGER: People hardly ever come here.

THE GUEST: But sometimes people come here.

THE VILLAGER: Yes. You're here.

THE GUEST: I came here ... well I guess you know why I came here.

THE VILLAGER: I think I do.

THE GUEST: I'm curious. Do you know much about the history of this room?

THE VILLAGER: I know people come here because a doctor is meant to appear here as a spirit, a doctor with a great reputation as a healer. People used to come here from miles around to see her when she was alive. She was also very wealthy, used to give money to ordinary people. So yes, people sometimes come here, to connect in some way with ...

THE GUEST: With the ghost?

THE VILLAGER: Yes. You could say that.

THE GUEST: I don't believe in such things, but I'll admit I've been curious about it.

THE VILLAGER: I've been here lots of times, but saw nothing, heard nothing.

THE GUEST: Just as I thought.

THE VILLAGER: I come here because it's peaceful.

THE GUEST: Yes, nothing to see here.

THE VILLAGER: Are you leaving?

THE GUEST: Yes, it's a dismal old place.

VOICE OF THE GHOST

Yes, you're right. I don't exist. There is nothing to see here. People sometimes comes here, my patients, my dear patients. I can't bear to see them suffering, so sometimes I help. But I'm not here, not how you understand it when people are meant to be somewhere. So please go, don't wait for me. I'm not here ... well sometimes I'm here, when I'm really needed. So yes, please go. Farewell. Goodbye. Don't tell anyone about me. I'm not really here.

THE END

I Am A Hologram was our attempt at humour and it did get laughs.

Judy was notable in playing a character based on herself. The humour was often centred around Margarita's role.

It was performed in-house - in the extension room at Shenehom.

I Am A Hologram

By the Shenehom Storytelling Group

THE SCENE: SHENEHOM CARE-HOME.
LONDON.

JUDY: Close the door please. We don't want anyone eavesdropping.

DENISE: We'll have to tighten things up. We've become careless.

MARGARITA: Thomas is not here. Where is he?

BALJIT: Why are there no biscuits?

JUDY: There was a plate of them here earlier.

MARGARITA: I ate them.

BALJIT: You ate all of them?

MARGARITA: Yes why not? So many hours in the day and so few biscuits.

JUDY: Yes, well we can have biscuits later. I guess we better start our meeting.

DENISE: There were biscuits in the kitchen last night but they disappeared. I think the guests had them.

BALJIT:: The paying guests or the other guests?

DENISE: Not sure.

JUDY: The non-paying guests, most likely.

BALJIT: I think we have digestive biscuits in the pantry.

JUDY: We better start. Time and tide.

MARGARITA: Yes let's get on with it. It's unbearable just sitting here like lemmings.

JUDY: Sorry, I'm doing my best. Shall we start with the AirBandB guests?

DENISE: We should wait until Thomas gets here. He does the bookings on the computer.

JUDY: We had a close shave last week. Agnes the cleaner was wondering who those two strange people having breakfast in the extension room were.

DENISE: I was there at the time. I told Agnes they were my visitors, family friends from South Africa.

MARGARITA: Good thinking. Last week one of the guests was walking out just as Gary was walking in.

BALJIT: What did you say?

MARGARITA: I said she's a Jehovah's witness.

DENISE: And he believed you?

JUDY: We've had a few close shaves lately. Surely one of these days they'll twig on.

MARGARITA: Thomas's here.

BALJIT: Hi Thomas.

THOMAS: Hi. How's everyone? (RINGS BELL) The meeting is hereby open.

DENISE: We're worried about the staff twigging on.

BALJIT: We've had a few close calls.

MARGARITA: The staff are not stupid. They must know what happens here at night.

THOMAS: You're right. We have a problem. I've just checked our AirBandB account and the reviews people are leaving are worrying. That couple we had from Chile left a review that said basically the accommodation wasn't bad but that there were too many animals in the corridors at night. And they said someone was hogging the bathroom in the morning.

DENISE: Judy's injured foxes and birds.

BALJIT: I brought a cat in one night. Just gave her some food and she followed me upstairs.

THOMAS: It's all good in principle, helping sick animals recover and hiding them in the home at night, but one of our AirBandB guests tripped over a lame fox in the corridor when they were going to the toilet at night.

JUDY: Yes we had two young foxes recovering for a few nights but they're gone now. I had them in Sally's old room.

THOMAS: We'll need Sally's old room if we're going to have any more paying guests. The home's filling up with new people.

BALJIT: I don't mind sleeping in the extension room and giving up my room to a guest, but not every night.

THOMAS: When the home had a few voids we made quite a bit of money from AirBandB guests but it's just not doable lately. The staff are becoming suspicious. They've seen people coming and going at strange times.

DENISE: They asked what that Spanish couple were doing having breakfast in the Shenehom kitchen.

JUDY: That was a close call. Luckily the Spanish guests couldn't speak a word of English.

THOMAS: It's too risky. They'll twig on. We'll have to do something else to make money.

DENISE: We need a distraction, something to take the staff's attention away from us.

BALJIT: Maybe we could start a fire in the back garden?

JUDY: Or start a riot out in the street?

MARGARITA: A riot in Barnes? Is that possible?

THOMAS: A distraction might not be a bad idea but I think from today we must stop smuggling guests in at night. It's too risky.

DENISE: Is it against the law?

BALJIT: I'm sure it is. It's a care-home not a guest-house. Technically speaking everything we do is against some law or other.

JUDY: Except eating and sleeping.

DENISE: Even sleeping in the wrong place can be against the law.

MARGARITA: How can we sleep in the wrong place?

DENISE: If you were to fall asleep in the middle of Piccadilly Circus someone would object.

MARGARITA: Why would I do that?

THOMAS: We're straying from the point, with all due respect. We must work out a new plan.

JUDY: Yes you're right. Times are changing. When Sally was in hospital I used her room to house two sick foxes. It was very handy.

THOMAS: They'll twig on eventually. They're not thick.

MARGARITA: They can be a bit thick at times.

BALJIT: They don't know what goes on here at night. They think everyone's asleep.

DENISE: Not always easy to sleep here at night. One night one of Judy's foxes was yelping for hours.

BALJIT: Yes those animals might be poorly but they don't half make a racket.

THOMAS: I think we should close our AirBandB account for now. We've already made a good bit of money. We should quit while we're ahead.

DENISE: The other guests are not such a problem.

BALJIT: I don't think the staff can see them.

DENISE: We can see them.

MARGARITA: I haven't see them.

JUDY: Well it can get a bit confusing here at times.

BALJIT: There was a terrible racket here last week. One of Judy's foxes was screeching into the wee hours.

JUDY: The poor thing. She'd hurt her foot.

THOMAS: It woke our paying guests. They were just about to write a bad review about it but I convinced them the foxes were out in the garden and had nothing to do with us.

DENISE: Bird poo in the bathroom. Foxes screeching at night. Maybe we've taken in enough animals for now.

JUDY: I was hoping for a bat.

BALJIT: Some animals are running up and down the stairs at night.

JUDY: Or a hedgehog.

THOMAS: We have no space for them anyhow. No room at the inn.

DENISE: What kind of diversion are we looking for?

THOMAS: A diversion might not be a bad idea, just to take the staff's attention away from us.

BALJIT: We could say something totally unexpected.

DENISE: Yes they think they know us so well, but do they really?

BALJIT: Chuck a smoke-bomb into the office the next time they are having a meeting.

MARGARITA: We don't want to get in trouble.

JUDY: Yes that's drastic.

THOMAS: We'll think of a diversion but in the meanwhile we have one final paying guest. And then we'll close our account with AirBandB.

DENISE: How much have we made from our paying guests?

THOMAS: Almost two grand. Not bad eh.

MARGARITA: Is it enough?

JUDY: It's a lot of money. The Wildlife Trust would be very happy to have it.

BALJIT: We can thank Thomas for organising it. Those computer classes you had with Gary really helped.

THOMAS: We worked it out together and I must say it's gone well.

DENISE: Ssssh. I think someone's coming.

JUDY: Not the police is it?

BALJIT: I don't think they'd call the police on us would they?

JUDY: I suppose it's a grave matter when viewed from a certain angle.

MARGARITA: We're not in trouble are we?

THOMAS: Well it's not the best is it, renting out spare rooms when the staff are not around and using the home as a sanctuary for sick animals.

BALJIT: Let's just sit here quietly and pretend we're meditating.

JUDY: Good idea. If anyone asks we'll say we're having an impromptu meditation group.

DENISE: I think they've gone, whoever they were.

JUDY: They're not our uninvited guests are they?

BALJIT: Hardly. It's too early.

THOMAS: I hope the uninvited guests are not worrying people.

DENISE: We just have to accept that the place is haunted.

JUDY: Charming isn't it.

BALJIT: I haven't seen them but I've heard them.

MARGARITA: What if the council find out the house is haunted. Will we get in trouble?

THOMAS: I don't think they care either way. They don't believe in ghosts.

JUDY: So if we don't believe in something, it doesn't exist?

MARGARITA: I don't believe in ghosts either but that doesn't mean they don't wander about the house at night.

BALJIT: One of them opened all the doors and windows one night and made the house very cold.

DENISE: I think that was me.

THOMAS: I don't know, it's weird. I mean if someone told me they have pains in their back or in their legs and they sounded plausible I'd probably believe them, even though I couldn't see the pains in question or experience them in any way.

BALJIT: Are the people in the council sceptics?

DENISE: There must be something wrong with them. If someone tells you they're experiencing something you'd usually believe them.

THOMAS: Politics. Someone high up the food-chain decided that ghosts don't exist.

BALJIT: According to Richmond Council you mean.

DENISE: I don't think our paying guests see them.

JUDY: Or the sick animals.

DENISE: We see them.

THOMAS: Anyhow, we're ahead. We only have one more guest, some guy visiting from Russia for only one night. After that we'll close our AirBandB account and nobody'll be any wiser. We done it, got away with it.

BALJIT: It feels good to get away with stuff.

JUDY: What about our night sanctuary for animals? I'd like to work with a badger with a wheezey chest if I can.

DENISE: Don't they bite?

BALJIT: Aren't they smelly?

JUDY: No they're totally safe. And not very smelly. This poor old fellow has a terrible chest.

THOMAS: No we have to suspend all activities for the moment. If we don't the staff will definitely twig on.

DENISE: Only one more guest.

BALJIT: I hope nothing goes wrong.

THOMAS: We might need a distraction.

JUDY: No fires in the back garden I hope.

MARGARITA: No. It would spread and burn the house down. We'd have to sleep on Barnes' Common for the rest of our lives.

THOMAS: We need a distraction for a few days, just to confuse the staff.

DENISE: Aren't they already confused?

BALJIT: Confuse them even more.

DENISE: I don't mind doing something radical for the cause.

JUDY: Not too radical I hope. We don't want to turn into anarchists.

THOMAS: It's making sense. One more guest for just one night. No more animals hiding in the home at night.

JUDY: They're not hiding as such, but rather recovering.

THOMAS: Hiding. Recovering. Whatever. Basically there's too much animal poo to deal with.

DENISE: And birdsong at odd times.

MARGARITA: I've got an idea.

BALJIT: And there was a very unusual noise here last night. Sounded like a cow mooing.

JUDY: I haven't gone that far, haven't smuggled a cow in.

BALJIT: Surely we haven't got room for livestock.

DENISE: Listen to Margarita. She's got an idea.

THOMAS: Go on Margarita, we're listening.

MARGARITA: You see the staff are used to seeing us in a certain way, very used to us as they've known us a long while. If we changed a bit they'd notice.

DENISE: Change in what way?

MARGARITA: If I said something entirely different to what I normally say when they ask me how I feel it'd throw them right off.

DENISE: Good idea. Say something bizarre.

JUDY: Go on Margarita, it sounds good.

MARGARITA: If I tell them I'm a hologram it'd get their attention.

JUDY: A hologram you say?

MARGARITA: Yes, I'm a hologram.

JUDY: It's different.

BALJIT: It might work.

DENISE: Would they buy it?

JUDY: It's good psychology.

THOMAS: Yes it might work. Do you think you could keep it up?

MARGARITA: I think I could, yes. I'll just say to them I'm a hologram, a hologram, a hologram a hologram.

DENISE: That'll get their attention.

BALJIT: You're not really a hologram are you?

DENISE: It's a strategy.

JUDY: A ploy.

DENISE: A play?

JUDY: No I said it's a ploy not a play.

MARGARITA: I am a hologram a hologram a hologram. I'm getting into this.

THOMAS: Okay, it's a plan.

JUDY: It's a ploy and a plan but not a play.

BALJIT: I can see you very clearly.

JUDY: She's not really a hologram.

DENISE: It's just a game, a distraction.

MARGARITA: I am a hologram a hologram a hologram.

BALJIT: She's a hologram.

JUDY: Whatever that's meant to be.

DENISE: Something that isn't real.

JUDY: Spiffing.

THOMAS: Good. I think we've found our distraction.

DENISE: So what are we going to do with the money we've saved from our paying guests?

BALJIT: Buy clothes.

THOMAS: We have a plan remember.

JUDY: Weren't we going to buy an away-day for the staff, just to get them out of our faces for a day?

BALJIT: That'd do. And once they're gone we'll have some fun.

DENISE: Me and Baljit were hoping we could spend it on clothes.

BALJIT: Shopping trip to Hammersmith.

JUDY: Or donate it to the Wetland Centre.

MARGARITA: I don't care either way, I'm not a materialist.

DENISE: We do need a break from the staff.

THOMAS: Okay, let's draw up a plan.

BALJIT: A cunning plan.

JUDY: I'm up for anything.

MARGARITA: I am a hologram.

DENISE: I'm a frustrated fashion-buyer.

BALJIT: Me too.

THOMAS: I'll cancel our AirBandB account, so no more guests. Denise you look after the guest when they arrive.

BALJIT: Our last guest. I'll help too.

THOMAS: Yes apparently it's some Russian guy by the name of Tutin or Butin or something like that. He sounds desperate.

JUDY: Sounds just the job for us.

THOMAS: Margarita, you distract the staff by pretending you're a hologram and Judy clean out what remains of our four-legged friends.

MARGARITA: Birds don't have four legs.

THOMAS: You know what I mean. Clean out what remains of their food and bedding.

JUDY: Consider it done.

THOMAS: Excellent.

JUDY: What could possibly go wrong?

MARGARITA: I'm not really a hologram am I?

BALJIT: No, you're pretending so as to distract staff.

MARGARITA: I'm worried that I might actually turn into one.

DENISE: Let us know if you do.

THOMAS: We'll get the staff packed off for an away-day and we'll have a bit of fun around here.

DENISE: No more sick animals, no more guests. End of an era.

JUDY: What about our other guests?

DENISE: Oh them.

THOMAS: Well if they're not bothering anyone we can leave them in peace.

DENISE: They bother me.

MARGARITA: I better go and harass the staff by telling them I'm a hologram.

THOMAS: It's lovely when a plan falls into place.

BALJIT: So what happens now?

DENISE: Time for lunch.

THOMAS: Any other business?

MARGARITA: I am a hologram a hologram a hologram a hologram.

THOMAS: The meeting is now over.

THE END

THE PEOPLE'S CO-OPERATIVE OF SHENEHOM

A one –act play performed by Shenehom Storytelling Group.

SCENE: Shenehom Care-Home Barnes. West London.

MARGARITA: Porcelain ginger jar, porcelain ginger jar. Raise the sails against the North winds. It's a happy day indeed. So much talk of freedom. We don't know what it all means, but who cares? Freedom is everything, isn't it? Who wouldn't wish to be free? Raise the jelly-fish. Hurrah for us. Hurrah for freedom!

JUDY: It's a capital idea really.

MARGARITA: It is.

THOMAS: We'll have to thrash out the details a bit more.

DENISE: We should just go for it.

JUDY: It'll take a bit of getting used to, I must admit.

MARGARITA: If we need a logo we should use the logo of a jellyfish. After all jellyfish have been living without a brain, without a heart and without blood for over 600 million years. That's what I call tenacity.

THOMAS: We'd have to work out details like medication and food.

DENISE: We can stick something in the microwave, or get takeaways.

JUDY: I'll continue to feed the birds and look after the wild-life.

MARGARITA: Let's hope nothing goes wrong?

THOMAS: If we're serious about it we'll have to change the locks and lock the staff out.

JUDY: Oh I forgot about them, what are we going to do about the staff?

MARGARITA: I don't want the staff to stop coming here.

THOMAS: We'll have to up our game.

DENISE: Can we have takeaways every evening?

JUDY: We could turn the extension room into a sanctuary for hungry foxes and homeless hedgehogs.

MARGARITA: I'm not sure. Suddenly it feels a bit wrong.

THOMAS: It could be interesting.

DENISE: We could get a hot-tub for the garden.

JUDY: Actually, do you think it'd be possible to get rid of the boundary wall in the garden? That would allow the wildlife from the common to come and go.

MARGARITA: I don't want our wall knocked down. We'd be on view to the world and anyone could come into the garden and look through the windows.

THOMAS: It's not impossible, but first things first.

DENISE: We could fly a flag from the roof, just to indicate that the house is liberated.

JUDY: The Jolly Rodger?

MARGARITA: If we really must fly a flag from the roof it should have a jellyfish on it.

THOMAS: We don't have to do anything. That's the point isn't it? Freedom.

DENISE: We could have parties every weekend.

JUDY: We could adopt a pony.

MARGARITA: Where would the pony live?

THOMAS: We'd have to work out a rota for chores.

DENISE: And the council. We'd have to nominate someone to deal with the council.

JUDY: We could erect stables out the back, nothing fancy.

MARGARITA: Stables for the pony to live in?

THOMAS: We'd have to figure out how this place works.

DENISE: I'm going to Hammersmith now. Let me know how it all goes.

MARGARITA: I don't think it's a good idea, for residents to take over Shenehom.

THOMAS: As I was saying, it' something we need to plan.

JUDY: Maybe we could turn the entire ground-floor into an animal sanctuary.

DENISE: Okay I'm off now, bye. You can work out the details when I'm away.

THOMAS: I have to go too. We can plan to take over the home later on.

MARGARITA: Where are you going?

JUDY: Is that it then?

THOMAS: We can close the meeting.

SCENE TWO:

MARGARITA: There's a strange man in the house.

DENISE: Oh yes I met him earlier. He's here about the pact.

MARGARITA: What pact?

DENISE: Apparently we have to sign up for some kind of pact.

MARGARITA: Why? I don't want to sign up to a pact with a strange man.

DENISE: It's something to do with us taking over the home, our rebellion.

MARGARITA: I don't like any of it. We haven't thought it through.

DENISE: Looks like it's going to happen soon. A flag on the roof declaring independence, changing the locks so as the staff can't get in.

MARGARITA: If we lock the staff out, who's going to take me to my appointment next week?

DENISE: One of us can go with you.

MARGARITA: You mean you'll go with me in the taxi?

DENISE: Why not?

MARGARITA: And wait for me?

DENISE: Sure.

MARGARITA: And then come back with me in the taxi.

DENISE: Yes.

MARGARITA: I don't want you to.

DENISE: Okay, we can work something out.

MARGARITA: I don't want that strange man to come with me either.

DENISE: I don't think he's planning to bring us out places. He's only here about the pact.

MARGARITA: I don't want to sign a pact with him either. Why is he wandering about the house on his own?

DENISE: I don't know. He looks like he knows what he's doing

MARGARITA: I don't like him. He was going against me earlier.

DENISE: We'll have to get used to a new routine around here, if

we're serious about declaring
independence and going it alone.

MARGARITA: I don't want to go
it alone.

DENISE: And make sacrifices.

MARGARITA: Sacrifices?

DENISE: We haven't worked it
out yet. The rebellion is only
beginning.

MARGARITA: I don't like any of
it. That man who wants us to sign
a pact is making me nervous. We
should call the rebellion off.

DENISE: Too late. We've crossed the Rubicon.

MARGARITA: Have we?

DENISE: Looks like it.

MARGARITA: How do you know?

DENISE: We had a meeting, declared independence, made certain arrangements. Looks like we're almost at the finishing post.

MARGARITA: I don't want to be almost at the finishing post. Can't we turn around and go back?

DENISE: Not sure. We've picked up a fair bit of wind in our sails. If we called it off now the others would be disappointed.

MARGARITA: Oh.

DENISE: Looks like we'll have to keep going.

MARGARITA: Does it?

DENISE: I'm sure it'll be fine once we get used to it.

MARGARITA: What's that man doing out in the garden?

DENISE: That's the man who's here about the pact?

MARGARITA: Why is he in the garden, looking in the window at us?

DENISE: I don't know. We should give him a wave.

MARGARITA: No don't wave at him. If we ignore him he might go away.

DENISE: He's has a good look around the entire house and the garden.

MARGARITA: I don't like him. I don't like any of this. I'm going upstairs.

DENISE: It's okay, he's gone.

MARGARITA: Let me know when it's all over, all this rebellion. I don't like it.

SCENE THREE

JUDY: So, you're here about a pact?

THOMAS: Yes. Nice to meet you.

JUDY: What kind of pact exactly?

THOMAS: Oh just the usual. I've brought the paperwork with me. You can read the small print if you like.

JUDY: I'm sure everything's in order. But as far as I'm aware we haven't requested a pact.

THOMAS: It's obligatory. As soon as you declared independence for the care-home you get to sign a pact.

JUDY: How remarkable. How did you hear about us?

THOMAS: It's all done through our office. They texted me on your address and said you're next to sign up.

JUDY: Really? How efficient.

THOMAS: We try. I've been doing it for so long it's become somewhat routine.

JUDY: And how much does this pact cost?

THOMAS: Money-wise, nothing.

JUDY: Nothing at all.

THOMAS: Nothing. You can sign now if you like.

JUDY: Okay, do you have a pen?

THOMAS: Yes, there you are. Sign there, on the dotted line.

JUDY: There you go.

THOMAS: That's lovely. Thank you.

JUDY: Great. So that's the pact all done and dusted.

THOMAS: Thank you I can send a copy in the post, for your records.

JUDY: You can stay for dinner.

THOMAS: No thank you, better make a move.

JUDY: By the way I forgot to ask, what exactly is the pact about?

THOMAS: Nothing much, nothing to worry about.

JUDY: Is it something to do with the council?

THOMAS: No, it's just to do with the human soul. A lot of people don't even believe we have a soul so these arrangements mean nothing to them. I guess people have so much to worry about these days, that they haven't got time to think about stuff like human souls.

JUDY: So how is declaring independence for our care-home connected to the human soul.

THOMAS: You're looking for freedom, and freedom comes with a cost. I'm afraid you can't expect to go independent and be free in the world as it stands without coming to an arrangement about your soul. It's nothing personal, just how things are. For those who don't believe in the soul it's a good deal as they're not losing anything.

JUDY: But what about those of us who do believe in a soul?

THOMAS: It's just how things stand I'm afraid. Personally I would say you're getting a pretty good deal. A number of our competitors are quite mercenary. Our reputation is pretty good, if I do say so myself.

JUDY: It's not something we've discussed. I don't know how the others feel about it.

THOMAS: You'll have time to study the contract. As I said, I'll send you on a copy in the post.

JUDY: We can't change our minds?

THOMAS: No sorry, you're all signed up.

JUDY: So we've signed our souls over to you. What do we get in return?

THOMAS: As it states in the contract, or the pact if you like, we have validated your freedom. We support your intentions. You see you must have at least one source who validates your freedom and your intentions. It's a natural law I'm sure. Or at least it should be.

JUDY: What about if we want our souls back?

THOMAS: Too late I'm afraid. It's all legal and correctly witnessed. Your souls officially belong to us.

JUDY: Oh dear.

THOMAS: Wouldn't worry about it if I were you. In the modern world a number of people don't even believe in the human soul. They have no interest in Plato or Aristotle's definition of the soul, or any other definition for that matter. It makes my job significantly easier.

JUDY: I do actually believe in the human soul.

THOMAS: That's fine. Your beliefs are entirely acceptable as far as we're concerned. Thankfully we live in a country where we are allowed to decide on our own private beliefs, within reason of course. Your beliefs are highly valued as far as we're concerned. As the situation now stands, we own your souls.

JUDY: I always assumed that God owns my soul.

THOMAS: Who or whatever you pledged your soul to prior to our arrangement is not strictly any concern of ours. As matters stand we now own your soul. We have your signature on an official and binding contract to prove it.

JUDY: Well, if you say so, but how would we go about getting our souls back? Is there some kind of form we'd need to fill in?

THOMAS: Sorry, it's totally binding. We must obey the property laws of England after all. It states that we own your souls for all eternity.

JUDY: All eternity sounds like a very long time.

THOMAS: Yes well that's the rules. I'm afraid we can't go around breaking the rules, can we?

JUDY: Do we have a judicial review?

THOMAS: Not when it comes to souls I'm afraid. Anyhow, I better get ready to go. There's a car coming to pick me up.

JUDY: It doesn't sound very promising for us, does it?

THOMAS: You can apply for an interest-free loan. We give out lots of loans actually. And we can send you out one of our life-style advisors. They can come here to the home. Free of charge. They have excellent ideas how to live.

JUDY: How to live without a soul?

THOMAS: You have a soul. It's just that's it is signed over to us.

JUDY: What's the name of your company?

THOMAS: Oh, here's my card. I really must go.

JUDY: Mr. Faust and Daughter. Purveyor of souls.

THOMAS: That's us. One of the oldest companies in the field. Really must go. Ta ra!

SCENE FOUR

MARGARITA: Freedom is a bit disappointing I must say. It doesn't feel any different than when we were not free.

JUDY: It's all quite new.

DENISE: Remember that old song?

THOMAS: The world is full of old songs.

MARGARITA: What old song?

DENISE: Can't remember who sang it. About freedom or something.

MARGARITA: Don't sing it. I couldn't bear it.

JUDY: Just one day into our new state of independence and already we've lost our souls. Not great is it?

THOMAS: We haven't got going yet. It's early days.

MARGARITA: Judy, why did you sign our souls away to that man?

JUDY: He seemed plausible.

DENISE: I think he duped us into signing that legal document. Hardly fair is it?

THOMAS: Life can be quite unfair, it seems.

MARGARITA: Yes well I'd like my soul back thank you very much.

JUDY: Seemingly we have souls, but they are owned by this man Faust.

MARGARITA: I've heard that when people don't have souls they can't see their reflection in the mirror. If I looked in the mirror in the morning and couldn't see my reflection I'd probably feel quite anxious.

DENISE: We could get rid of all the mirrors in the home.

JUDY: It's all gone rather flat. One minute we were planning all manner of marvellous things such as turning the ground-floor of the home into an animal sanctuary, and now we're wondering if we'll be able to even see ourselves in the mirror.

THOMAS: I think it's got to do with freedom. The more freedom, the more hassle.

DENISE: People often don't like thinking for themselves. It's easier to follow instructions.

JUDY: So much for freedom.

MARGARITA: I don't like any of it. That man who came here gave me the creeps.

THOMAS: It makes sense. After all he's in the business of buying souls.

MARGARITA: Very creepy. I feel like going up to my room and staying there until all this is over.

DENISE: I'm off to Hammersmith soon.

THOMAS: We'll have to resolve all this. If we're going ahead with independence we may have to accept that we won't be in control of our souls.

DENISE: We got nothing tangible from Faust. Nothing we can take out now and then and look at.

MARGARITA: We signed our souls away for nothing. And I'm really beginning to miss my soul.

THOMAS: Not exactly. They are validating our freedom and our independence. If we're not validated in the world how can we say we exist?

JUDY: Well they could have validated us at a lesser cost. We all could have chipped in a fiver let's say.

DENISE: Typical salesman.

MARGARITA: When can I have my soul back?

THOMAS: We can still continue without control of our souls. It doesn't mean we have to call off the rebellion. We shouldn't be put off by the first little problem that comes along.

JUDY: It's hardly a little problem to be fair, I mean we only have one human soul, as far as I'm aware.

DENISE: A soulless rebellion.

MARGARITA: We haven't factored in anxiety.

JUDY: Or animal rights.

THOMAS: We can draw up a new agenda.

DENISE: What's a human soul among friends?

THOMAS: Someone's coming.

MARGARITA: It's Gary.

DENISE: Hi Gary.

GARY: Hi. How is everyone?

MARGARITA: Some weird man came here and Judy signed our souls away to him.

JUDY: We tried to go independent, but it didn't work out very well.

THOMAS: It's all got to do with the cost of freedom. Seemingly it's quite costly.

GARY: Do you mean that guy who was here earlier?

MARGARITA: The weird man.

JUDY: From Faust and Daughter.

THOMAS: He's a legal fellow.

DENISE: A purveyor of souls.

GARY: He tried to pull a quick one. Tried to say he now owns all the resident's souls. He showed me a dodgy contract but I wasn't having it. I just snapped it out of his hands and tore it up.

MARGARITA: You tore it up?

DENISE: So we don't have a pact with him?

GARY: Not likely. All done and dusted.

JUDY: So we have our souls back?

GARY: Absolutely. I escorted that chancer off the premises and please ignore everything he said.

MARGARITA: Great. We have our souls back.

THOMAS: What about our freedom?

GARY: You have as much freedom as the laws of nature grant you.

JUDY: It's a spiffing deal.

DENISE: Hurrah for Gary.

MARGARITA: Down with freedom. Up with the laws of nature.

GARY: To celebrate we're having a takeaway this evening.

DENISE: Great. Indian?

JUDY: Chinese?

MARGARITA: Italian?

THOMAS: Things are looking up. We're on the subject of food again.

GARY: We'll work something out.

THE END

CLEVER TREVOR

(a one-act play)

By the Shenehom Storytelling Group

DR FRY: Judy.

DENNIS: Thomas.

JOANIE: Denise.

JANIE: Baljit.

JAZZY: Margarita.

SCENE ONE

A psychiatrist's office, West London.

DR FRY: So Dennis ... how are we?

DENNIS: Uh ... I don't know.

DR FRY: Okay. Take your time. You don't know.

DENNIS: I don't know how we are, how would I? I know how I am, I think.

DR FRY: Okay, let me rephrase the question. How are you?

DENNIS: I'm okay, I guess.

DR FRY: Good, so we're off to a jolly start. And how are you getting on with everyone?

DENNIS: Everyone?

DR FRY: When I say everyone, I mean everyone in the home where you live.

DENNIS: It's a not a home, it's shared accommodation.

DR FRY: Okay, so how are you getting on with everyone, in your shared accommodation?

DENNIS: Pretty good, as far as I'm aware.

DR FRY: You don't have family as far as I remember, so it must be nice to have the people you live with to talk to.

DENNIS: Family don't really want to know me, not since that accident.

DR FRY: What accident? As far as I remember there were quite a few.

DENNIS: I burnt the family house to the ground.

DR FRY: Ah yes, that accident. Luckily there was nobody at home.

DENNIS: Yes ... I was having a bad day, as far as I can recall.

DR FRY: I see. Well we don't want you isolated, do we? Do you have any friends where you live, someone you can confide in?

DENNIS: Trevor's my best friend.

DR FRY: Good. And what sort of things does Trevor like doing?

DENNIS: I don't think he's got any special interests. He sleeps a lot. Sometimes he chases pigeons out in the back garden.

DR FRY: How intriguing. And why does he chase pigeons?

DENNIS: I don't know. He never mentions it. Some days he sits on the garden wall, just watching the pigeons. He just sits there, watching them. He obviously gets something out of it.

DR FRY: Do the staff who manage the shared accommodation know about Trevor? Do they know he sits on the garden wall, watching pigeons?

DENNIS: Yes, I'm sure they do. One staff member likes Trevor. And sometimes strokes his neck.

DR FRY: Oh really. A member of staff strokes your friend Trevor's neck?

DENNIS: Yes. Sometimes the same member of staff scratches Trevor's belly. Some days Trevor is really friendly and up for a bit of physical contact. Other days he just watches the pigeons in the back garden.

DR FRY: So Trevor lives in your shared accommodation too?

DENNIS: Yes. He likes to sleep in the bin-shed. Sometimes he sleeps under my bed.

DR FRY: Really? How interesting. Remember in the past when we spoke about the difference between imaginary people, and real people?

DENNIS: Trevor is real. He's my pet cat.

DR FRY: Oh he's a cat.

DENNIS: Yes he's my pet, a ginger tabby. Did you think I was talking about an imaginary person?

DR FRY: I'm glad to hear you have a pet tabby. Do you take care of him, feed him, take him to the vet, or do you need help from the staff?

DENNIS: I take care of Trevor. He's my cat.

DR FRY: Great. So apart from your cat do you talk to anyone at the scheme where you live?

DENNIS: Yes.

DR FRY: Good. So, you're getting on well brighter. Wouldn't you say it's looking brighter?

DENNIS: Yes. It's looking brighter.

DR FRY: You were having quite bad hand tremors the last time we met.

DENNIS: Side effects from medication, you said.

DR FRY: But look at your hands now. No tremors.

DENNIS: Yes, I had some advice and it really helped.

DR FRY: Advice? Excellent. From the staff at the scheme where you live?

DENNIS: I don't know if I should talk about it just now Doctor Fry.Maybe we could talk about it some other day.

DR FRY: You can trust me Dennis. We've spoken about many things in the past. It's important we trust each other.

DENNIS: Yes, but ...

DR FRY: But what? You clearly got some really good advice. Where's the harm in talking about it?

DENNIS: The last time we spoke in an honest way, do you remember what happened?

DR FRY: Not really. What happened?

DENNIS: You said I was delusional and sent me to hospital, in an ambulance.

DR FRY: That was a long time ago Dennis. That was before we sorted out your meds. Nothing like that could happen today.

DENNIS: It wasn't all that long ago.

DR FRY: I can assure you anything that you say will be respected and held in confidence. You know you can trust me.

DENNIS: Okay ... the advice came from ...

DR FRY: Go on Dennis. You can tell me. Where did you get such good advice from?

DENNIS: From Trevor.

DR FRY: From Trevor, your pet cat?

DENNIS: Yes, from Trevor. I know he's just a cat, but I think he's an unusual cat.

DR FRY: How so?

DENNIS: He knows stuff. And he's telepathic. I guess a lot of animals are telepathic, to one degree or other. Trevor definitely is.

DR FRY: Really?

DENNIS: He knows when people are poorly and need to see a doctor, for example.

DR FRY: How extraordinary.

DENNIS: He'll appear in your room and when you wake, he'll be there, staring at you. If you wake up and Trevor's staring at you, it's time to make an appointment to see a doctor.

DR FRY: A medical cat?

DENNIS: That's just one way Trevor tells us stuff.

DR FRY: Intriguing.

DENNIS: Trevor surprises us all the time. He tunes into some kind of field of energy or communication, or something like that ... somewhere very different to here.

DR FRY: And he talks to you directly?

DENNIS: Trevor can't talk. He's a cat.

DR FRY: So he communicates non-verbally?

DENNIS: Yes. What other way could he communicate?

DR FRY: Just asking Dennis, just asking. Well wellwell. Just look at the time. Don't the minutes fly by?

DENNIS: It's funny you should say that, as Trevor has a theory that time is speeding up. I know it's not his idea entirely. I know lots of clever people have similar ideas. But Trevor really believes in it.

DR FRY: And he communicated that to you through telepathy?

DENNIS: No, actually he told me all that in a dream. Now and then when Trevor has something important to say he appears in my dreams and speaks to me in person.

DR FRY: What a remarkable cat.

DENNIS: He is. He's really passionate on the subjects close to his heart, like animal welfare and the Red Cross. He can be very convincing.

DR FRY: I'm sure. Well I think that's all for today Dennis. Time and tide.

DENNIS: Time and tide what?

DR FRY: Just an old saying. Time and tide wait for no man.

DENNIS: I see.

DR FRY: Bye for now. I'll be in touch.

Scene two

A shared accommodation scheme. West London.

JOANIE: It's terrible.

JANIE: We should visit.

JAZZY: It's disconnected from reality.

JOANIE: Why is it disconnected from reality?

JAZZY: Not sure. I just said that as I couldn't think of anything else to say.

JANIE: What hospital?

JOANIE: Queen Mary's.

JAZZY: Queen Mary's. I broke the record there for eating extra portions of ice-cream.

JANIE: I will visit tomorrow.

JOANIE: It's terrible, dragging someone into hospital like that.

JAZZY: Did they drag him?

JOANIE: No, not literally.

JANIE: I'll bring him cake.

JAZZY: What kind of cake?

JANIE: Lemon drizzle.

JOANIE: He likes treacle tarts.

JAZZY: Can we have lemon drizzle cake too?

JANIE: I'll bring him crisps. Walker's salt and vinegar he likes.

JAZZY: I like Genoa cake.

JOANIE: It's terrible, putting him in hospital like that.

JAZZY: Why did they put him in hospital?

JANIE: The doctor put him there. Doctor Fry.

JOANIE: I don't like Doctor Fry. There's something creepy about her.

JAZZY: I don't know her. I used to know a doctor called Doctor Kevin Doom.

JANIE: Doctor Doom.

JAZZY: And when I was in hospital the woman in the next bed believed she was a former prime minister. And the name of the psychiatrist on the ward was Dr Theresa May.

JOANIE: I had a nurse called Nurse Marie Fang.

JAZZY: Did she actually have a fang?

JOANIE: We're forgetting about Dennis. He's in hospital remember.

JANIE: I haven't forgotten. I'll visit tomorrow.

JOANIE: Dennis hasn't been the same since he read that book that was lying around.

JAZZY: What book?

JOANIE: The one that was lying around.

JANIE: Yes, he read that book from cover to cover. It was about sorrow.

JAZZY: The Sorrows of Young Werther.

JOANIE: He took it to heart.

JANIE: Who is going to look after Trevor?

JAZZY: Trevor won't like it. He hates to be separated from Dennis.

JANIE: I seen Trevor, out on the garden wall, watching the pigeons.

JOANIE: Trevor's a special cat, very sensitive.

JANIE: Trevor saved your life.

JOANIE: He did. He followed me around for an entire week. Everywhere I went Trevor was there. One morning I woke up in bed and he was sitting on my head, miaowing very loudly.

JAZZY: He does that to people who are poorly.

JOANIE: He hassled me so much I went to the doctor and they found a bleed on my brain. They said it could have killed me.

JAZZY: He saved you.

JANIE: Trevor can be naughty too. Once he killed a pigeon and put the dead pigeon on my pillow.

JAZZY: That's a sign he likes you.

JANIE: The pigeon's eye got stuck in my hair.

JOANIE: Okay, let's organise ourselves. We have to visit Dennis, and then maybe a find a way of getting him out of there. And then we have to make sure Trevor is okay. He's an unusual cat after all.

JAZZY: If we are getting cake, we should get double chocolate instead of lemon drizzle.

JOANIE: Hold on. What about if we talk about all the weird stuff Trevor can do and we get in trouble?

JAZZY: Is Dennis in trouble?

JANIE: Maybe we shouldn't talk about Trevor to other people, at all.

JOANIE: It sounds like a plan. If anyone asks us about Trevor we'll just say he's an ordinary tabby, without any special skills at all.

JAZZY: Why do we have to tell lies?

JANIE: It's not telling lies. We're just not talking about Trevor when other people are around.

JAZZY: We could hide Trevor until it all blows over, lock him in the bin-shed.

JOANIE: Let's keep it simple. If anyone mentions Trevor, we know nothing.

JANIE: We'll say Trevor is just a normal cat.

JOANIE: Agreed. From here on in Trevor is not clever at all.

JAZZY: Not clever Trevor, just boring old normal Trevor.

JANIE: Agreed.

SCENE THREE

JAZZY: It's Dennis.

JANIE: We thought you were in hospital.

JOANIE: Did you escape?

DENNIS: Hi, how is everyone? And no, I didn't escape. They released me.

JANIE: I was going to bring you crisps.

JOANIE: Why did they release you so soon?

JAZZY: When I was in there they didn't release me so soon.

DENNIS: I'd like to think it was all a mistake.

JAZZY: They kept me there for ages.

JANIE: Trevor missed you.

JOANIE: We all missed you.

JAZZY: I didn't miss you, as you weren't gone long enough.

JANIE: Why did they let you out so early?

DENNIS: I spent only one night there. The next morning during a ward-round a psychiatrist asked me question after question and I answered all the questions correctly, so the psychiatrist said I'm free to go.

JAZZY: They said you were free to go? They didn't say that to me. I had to beg them to let me out.

JANIE: How did you know what to say?

DENNIS: You might take a guess.

JOANIE: Don't say it's got something to do with a certain cat?

JANIE: Did Trevor take the bus to the hospital?

JAZZY: Can a cat travel free on the bus?

DENNIS: Actually, Trevor communicated with me telepathically. Told me to tell the psychiatrist I'd forgotten to take my mood-stabilizer, and when I do that it makes me a bit confused. But once I'm fully back on my meds, I don't confuse reality with fantasy.

JAZZY: Reality is over-rated.

JOANIE: And it worked?

DENNIS: It worked.

JANIE: Trevor saved the day.

DENNIS: He did. He knows that if you talk about how successful meds are to psychiatrists they like it. They can cope with a lapse in thinking due to forgetting to take meds. They can't cope with telepathic cats.

JANIE: So, you're free?

DENNIS: I guess so.

JOANIE: Well done Dennis. Well done Trevor.

JAZZY: Where is Trevor?

JANIE: He's sitting on the garden wall, staring at the pigeons again.

JAZZY: Why does Trevor stare at the pigeons so much?

JOANIE: If you wait long enough, he might tell you. Isn't that right Trevor.

DENNIS: Maybe. If he feels it's important enough he might appear in your dreams and tell you about why he stares at the pigeons.

JOANIE: What a strange cat.

JAZZY: Janie, can we have that cake you were going to bring to Dennis?

JANIE: It's all gone. I ate it.

JAZZY: What, all of it?

JANIE: Yes, all gone. The crisps are gone too.

JOANIE: Never mind, cake isn't everything.

DENNIS: That's right, cake is over-rated, almost as much as psychiatrists are over-rated.

JAZZY: I'm not so sure.

JOANIE: Three cheers for Dennis!

JANIE: Three cheers for Trevor!

JAZZY: Three cheers for cake!

SCENE FOUR

DR FRY: Hi, this is Doctor Annabel Fry. I'm afraid I won't be in today. I've been sneezing all morning. I've got a cat allergy and it feels as if a cat has gotten into my bedroom. That's a ridiculous idea I know, as I would not allow a cat to come within a mile of here. Strange isn't it. So, I won't be in today as my eyes and nose are streaming. A cat allergy with no cat in sight. How very odd. Anyhow, bye for now.

THE END

The following poems were written in-house and recited by residents at a poetry event in the home and a second poetry event at the Old Sorting Office theatre in West London.

A Visitor

The tail stuck out

From underneath my bedroom furniture.

To begin with I wasn't quite sure

If I'd like to share my tidy bedroom

With one who had such a suspicious-looking tail.

Such co-operation would surely fail.

Irrespective of the strange fellow's character,

his or her pluses or minuses

whether they suffer from bad breath or sinuses

I'm afraid I must conclude,

I have doubts about someone with grey fur

And who scampers off whenever I move.

Our conversations would be rather one-sided

And it wouldn't be easy to hide it,

The tail I mean.

Once seen it can't be unseen.

Not wishing to shout it from the roof of the house

But I object to sharing my room with a mouse.

Margarita

Beating Gary at Chess

I didn't play exceptionally well,

I've played better.

A random pawn was played too quickly,

As far as I could tell.

It rained a lot that day

As far as I remember.

But I digress.

Because on that day

I beat Gary at chess.

Thomas

The dots of love

My life is a series of dots
that when joined together

weigh as light as a
feather,

upon my heart.

The dots start in India

and extend across great
oceans to

a dear sister in Canada.

And they wind their way
to a beloved

daughter in Sunbury.

They are here too, in
Shenehom.

The dots of connection
blessed from above,

that when joined together
spell the word 'love.'

Baljit

A Prickly Friend

The hedgehog is a mammal

But is also my friend.

Not as thirsty as a camel

But we cannot pretend

That he's any less of a fellow

Or that he's not as important as you
and I.

His views on politics are quite
mellow.

And he understands maths to the
standard of Pi.

You'll like him I guarantee

For I've invited him this evening for tea.

Judy Tanner

Lines for A Friend

The happiest times are in acceptance.

Accepting ourselves and others.

I remember you easily.

The mildest of shudders.

A word remembered.

As if something of you passed by.

On the stairway or in the kitchen,

where we sat of an evening.

You'd say something unfunny.

But somehow it was funny.

A pause. Gesture. A dry cough.

Yes eat it all up. Go on. Eat it all.

In acceptance there's a certain love.

If you'd like such a word. You probably
wouldn't

But anyhow. If we substitute a word for love.

Something neutral, it might please you.

We accepted each other.

That's easier than saying much more.

I guess we had our own code.

Our own way of inhabiting each other's spaces.

Here, take me by the arm old friend.

Lead me down destiny road.

Margarita

A Journey

People taking notes,

wearing white coats.

The past often wasn't great,

measured by deficits of hate.

But now my room's a boutique.

My taste in fashion unique.

I haven't yet visited Rio or
Montevideo

but I've come a long way since
Bulowayo.

Denise

Porcelain Ginger Jar

This is me, who I am.

I was once a mystery to myself and others,

But not now.

Now I know who I am,

and mostly love who I am.

Can I tell you about a perfect moment,

what a perfect moment means to me?

And how such moments are icing on a cake

that's never past it's sell-by date.

Summer. Evening. Maybe August.

Everyone loves August.

It's almost impossible to be offended by August.

Garden. Think of it.

Think of a garden in August.

Here in Barnes, our Barnes,

the Barnes that holds us tenderly in its lightest embrace.

Garden. August. A blue sky.

There's a fairy-garden too and a raven

frowning from his perch on the fence.

It's one of those good-natured ravens

that wouldn't dream of going against me,

or going against anyone.

Mister Raven likes August too,

despite his frown

and the gown of black

nature has painted him in.

Planes crossing the perfect sky

are people and numbers

Sevenish. A keyworker from Shenehom's past.

Heathrow-bound. Friends.

Did the pilot just dip his wings to say hello?

Someone on the radio once said that life is a bad
half an hour,

peppered with exquisite moments.

Upstairs there's a porcelain ginger-jar

Guarding the space where I sleep.

August stretches out lazily before us,

and there's always the hope of more exquisite
moments.

Or friendliness or kindness or understanding.

Or just kindness.

MARGARITA

Jerusalem

Hammersmith is my Jerusalem,

my Alpha and Omega.

The place where I go in my heart

when the world turns grey.

Beadon Road. Bridge Avenue. Yesterday's
goodbyes.

My bridge of sighs.

Once I was in Starburger on King Street

with a friend who walked very lightly through
the world.

And it felt as if the earth stopped turning

and we were frozen there in time,

outside gravity.

And then after a minute or so the earth started
turning again

and the natural laws settled on us

like the latest cardboard-recycling regulations
from the council.

It's hard to forget stuff like that.

Hard to forget there was such a time and such a
place.

Hammersmith is my 'Strictly' where I dance in
my spirit.

And I'm amazed when people ask me why I go
there so often,

or why I love going there.

We all need a Hammersmith, somewhere to go

when life falls away from us and what life might
be

stands up on its hind-legs right in front of us.

Are you my Hammersmith?

Will you help me find my way there?

DENISE

The Bridge

The bridge begins

somewhere in our soul

and ends at Digby Mansions.

A workman fell off it once.

The 1990s I think.

He didn't make it.

But I did.

I came from a dark place

to the other side,

wearing much the same face

and in the same old style.

Another inch, another mile.

Hammersmith Bridge in the morning

And me walking over it.

Crossing an immense span of time

from when hardly anything happened

To when there's so much more.

I've become my own friend

and a friend to others.

My door opens freely at the lightest
touch

And I don't have many problems as
such.

On the bridge, in the morning.

Crossing this immensity of time.

Moving forward, always trying.

Living in a room where the door is unlocked

and where the road ahead is not blocked.

THOMAS

The Future

Hope is a horoscope

that outburns the sun.

Healing is kneeling

with void hands.

Recovery is freedom

from want and wealth.

Faith is the soul

decked out for the day ahead.

Love is a sun-flower among

small-sphered flowers in the stars.

Peace is the magic of strange hours

and the scent of Spring flowers.

Dreams are sprinkled with the sparks of
perfect fire

and noble notions of the higher.

These passing moments

are the rooted things that grow between us.

The future is something we have yet to atone
for.

A Vision

I saw a vision -

fluff tangled in her hair.

In her hands she held

pools of tears cried by the dead.

She begged me not to worship

an extinct fire.

She said she'd always been with me.

I said always?

She said yes.

Always.

And I'm with you until

the wreck and ruin

of what once was great -

my fetters are forged by fate.

Who are you? I asked.

I'm time's grey pillar.

I'm the mark of a wine-red hand.

I'm everything that isn't shameful.

I'm your guardian angel.

Here, we live.

I walked through temples

stripped of their purple and ermine.

Past weeping faces of the weary

and gold gowns made not by man.

A stream led to the sea.

The sea led me here.

A swimmer passed like an arrow of death

or a shaft of light.

I woke in my room

overlooking the garden

And the faery-garden.

A garden within a garden.

I slumbered in the arms of recovery

and woke in a spell.

At night I dream of sun-coloured lands.

Who can measure the heights of such thought?

On the altar of the moment

the years are but dust.

Here, we hold life up to our

lips and laugh.

Here, we mix the night-winds with humour.

Here, we live like kings and queens

with blood-red fruit in our hands.

Here, we live.

PEOPLE TELL ME MY FACE MAKES THEM THINK ABOUT A FLYING SAUCER.

WHICH TELLS ME HOW MANY PEOPLE BELIEVE IN FANTASY RATHER THAN TAKING PEOPLE AT FACE VALUE.

IT CAN BE BORING HERE AT TIMES... SOME OF US REALLY LIKE THE SHENEHOM GROUPS. SO GOOD JOB, KEEP RUNNING THEM.
YEAH. BORING.

Printed in Poland
by Amazon Fulfillment
Poland Sp. z o.o., Wrocław
17 July 2023

c8fe5b09-1668-4c09-8e2e-878169592a74R01